PIANO STANDARDS

20 Jazz Gems from the Early 20th Century

ARRANGED BY PHILLIP KEVEREN

— PIANO LEVEL —
INTERMEDIATE TO ADVANCED

ISBN 978-1-70516-762-5

HAL•LEONARD®

Visit Hal Leonard Online at
www.halleonard.com

Visit Phillip at
www.phillipkeveren.com

World headquarters, contact:
Hal Leonard
7777 West Bluemound Road
Milwaukee, WI 53213
Email: info@halleonard.com

In Europe, contact:
Hal Leonard Europe Limited
42 Wigmore Street
Marylebone, London, W1U 2RY
Email: info@halleonardeurope.com

In Australia, contact:
Hal Leonard Australia Pty. Ltd.
4 Lentara Court
Cheltenham, Victoria, 3192 Australia
Email: info@halleonard.com.au

PREFACE

This collection of songs came together, originally, as a piano solo recording project for Burton Avenue Music. When I received the song list (assembled by veteran music executive, Greg Howard), he included YouTube links to help me get my head around the material. Many of the recordings featured Beegie Adair (legendary jazz pianist) and Jaimee Paul (stellar vocal stylist). I highly recommend "After the Ball," an album you can find in all the digital outlets. The musicianship is inspiring, and it will help in your preparation to play the settings in this folio.

The songwriters behind these tunes knew their stuff. You will recognize Irving Berlin and George Gershwin, while other names will be less familiar. The common thread through all of these compositions is excellence. Melodies that soar, harmonies that resonate, and rhythms that set toes to tapping – all in abundance here.

I hope you enjoy this collection of terrific songs!

Sincerely,

Phillip Keveren

BIOGRAPHY

Phillip Keveren, a multi-talented keyboard artist and composer, writes original works in a variety of genres from piano solo to symphonic orchestra. He gives frequent concerts and workshops for teachers and their students in the United States, Canada, Europe, and Asia. Mr. Keveren holds a B.M. in composition from California State University Northridge and a M.M. in composition from the University of Southern California.

CONTENTS

AFTER THE BALL

Words and Music by CHARLES K. HARRIS
Arranged by Phillip Keveren

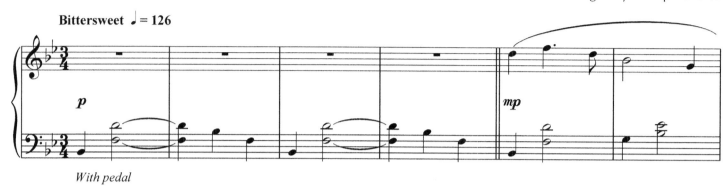

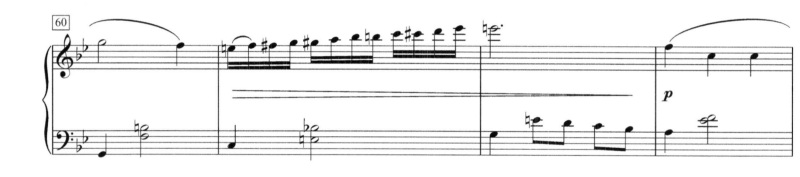

AFTER YOU'VE GONE

Words by HENRY CREAMER
Music by TURNER LAYTON
Arranged by Phillip Keveren

ALL ALONE

Words and Music by IRVING BERLIN
Arranged by Phillip Keveren

Tenderly ♩= c. 104

With pedal

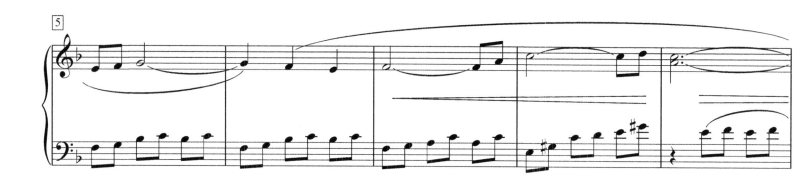

ALWAYS

Words and Music by IRVING BERLIN
Arranged by Phillip Keveren

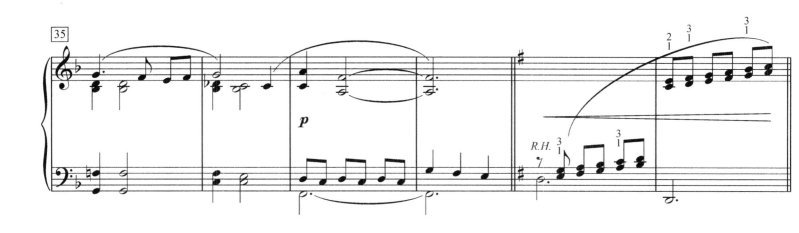

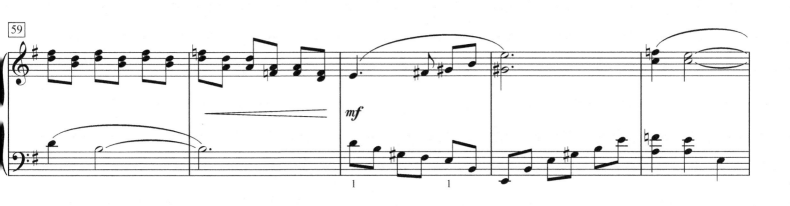

DO IT AGAIN

Words by B.G. DeSYLVA
Music by GEORGE GERSHWIN
Arranged by Phillip Keveren

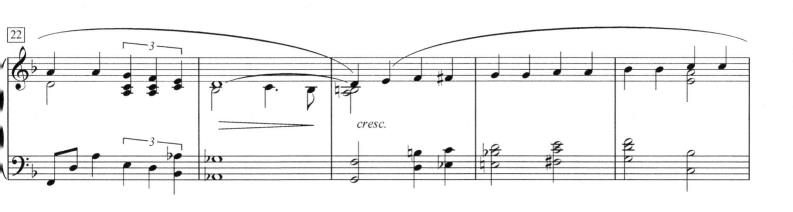

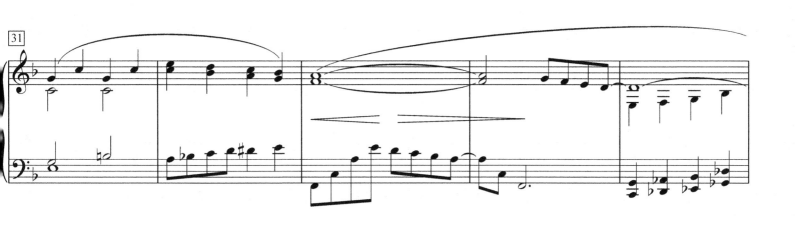

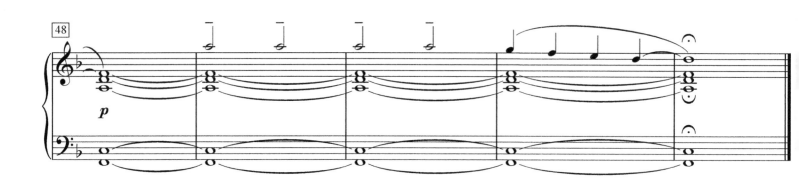

FASCINATION
(Valse Tzigane)

By F.D. MARCHETTI
Arranged by Phillip Keveren

Tenderly ♩ = c. 100

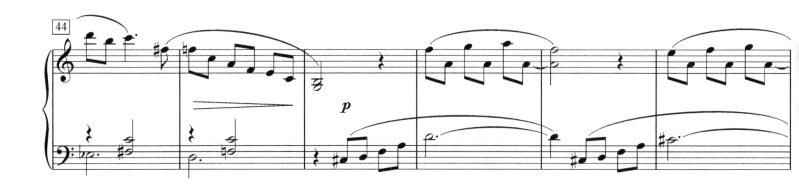

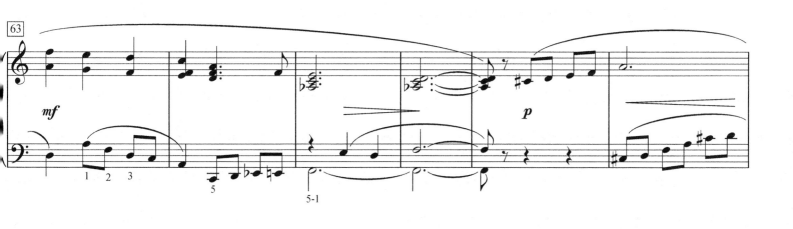

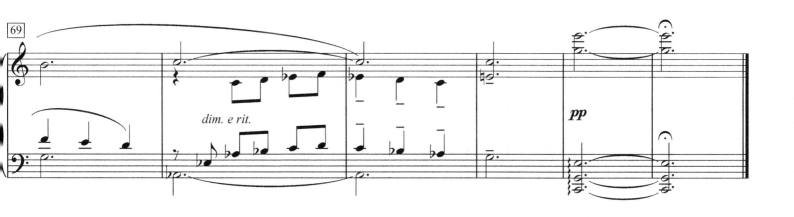

I WONDER WHO'S KISSING HER NOW

Lyrics by WILL M. HOUGH and FRANK R. ADAMS
Music by JOSEPH E. HOWARD and HAROLD ORLOB
Arranged by Phillip Keveren

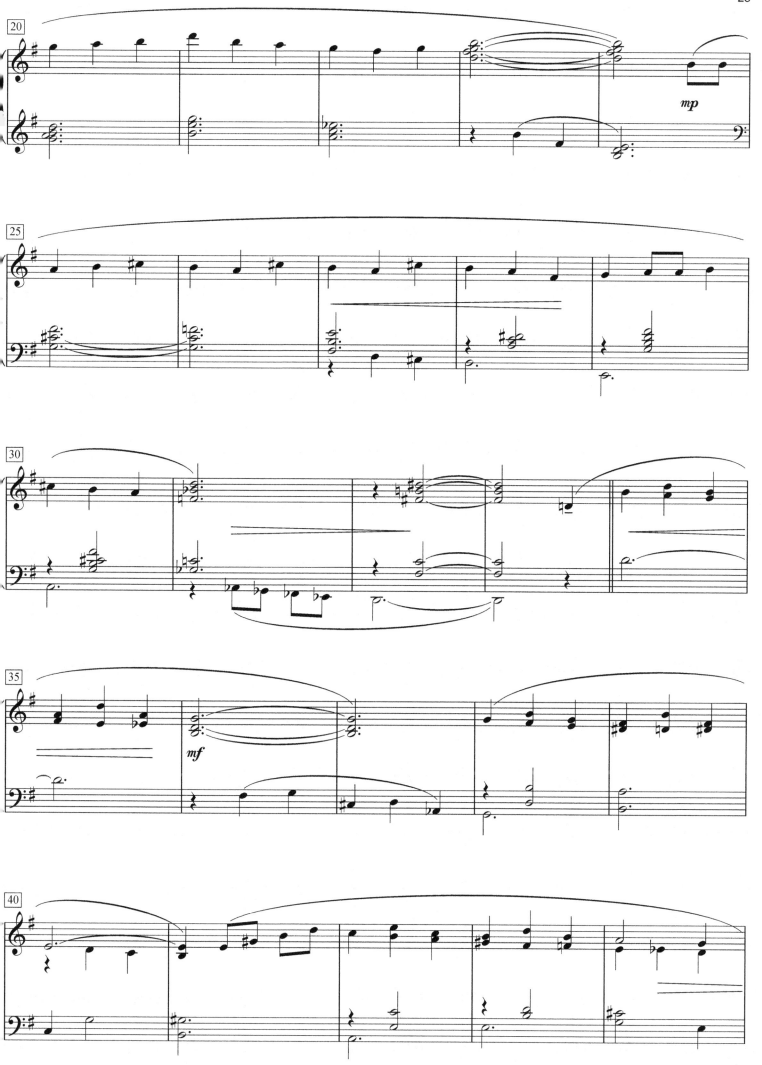

MANHATTAN

Words by LORENZ HART
Music by RICHARD RODGERS
Arranged by Phillip Keveren

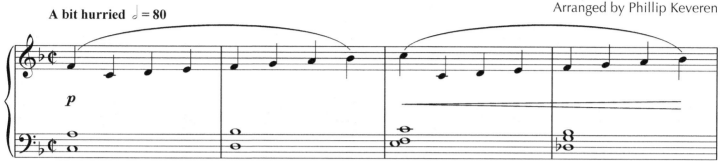

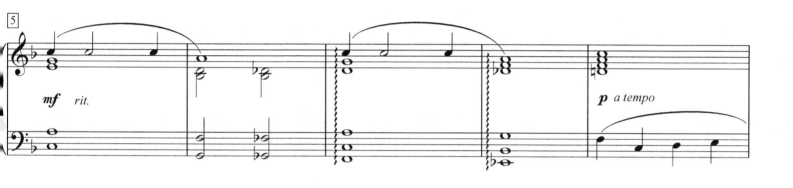

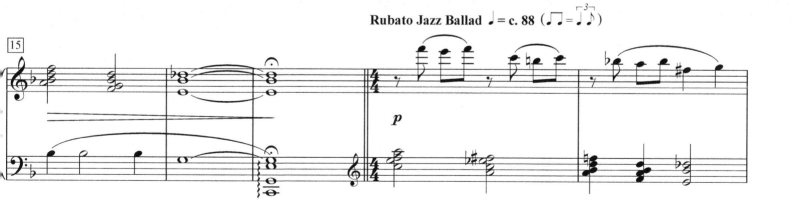

I'M ALWAYS CHASING RAINBOWS

Words by JOSEPH McCARTHY
Music by HARRY CARROLL
Arranged by Phillip Keveren

OH, LADY BE GOOD!

Words and Music by GEORGE GERSHWIN
and IRA GERSHWIN
Arranged by Phillip Keveren

POOR BUTTERFLY

Words by JOHN L. GOLDEN
Music by RAYMOND HUBBELL
Arranged by Phillip Keveren

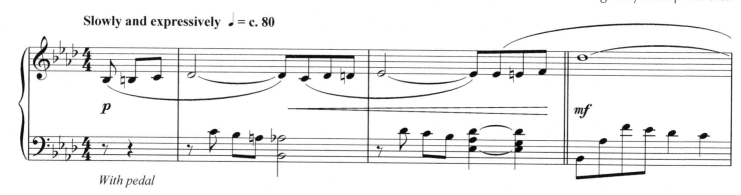

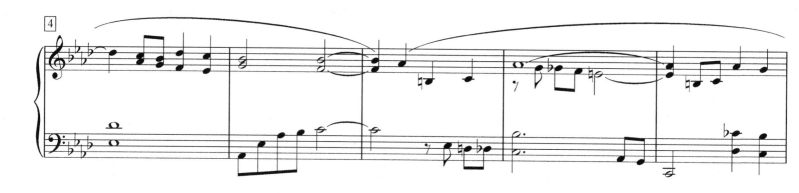

A PRETTY GIRL IS LIKE A MELODY

Words and Music by IRVING BERLIN
Arranged by Phillip Keveren

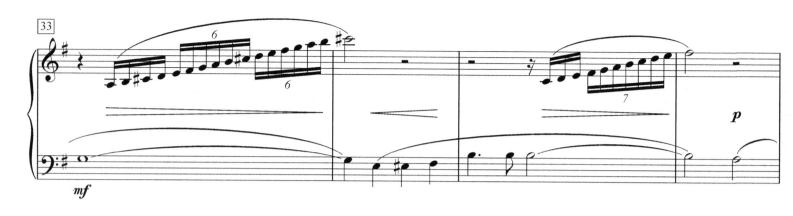

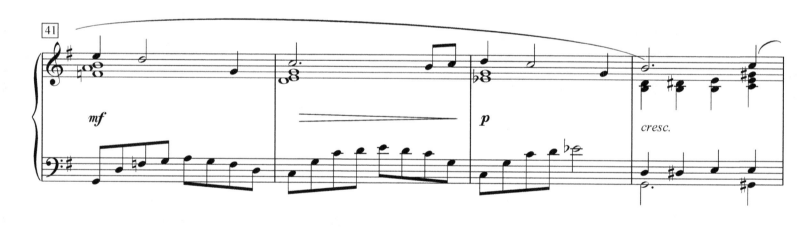

REMEMBER

Words and Music by IRVING BERLIN
Arranged by Phillip Keveren

Tentatively, with rubato ♩ = c. 84

41

SHINE ON, HARVEST MOON

Words by JACK NORWORTH
Music by NORA BAYES
and JACK NORWORTH
Arranged by Phillip Keveren

SOMEBODY LOVES ME

Words by B.G. DeSYLVA
and BALLARD MacDONALD
Music by GEORGE GERSHWIN
Arranged by PHILLIP KEVEREN

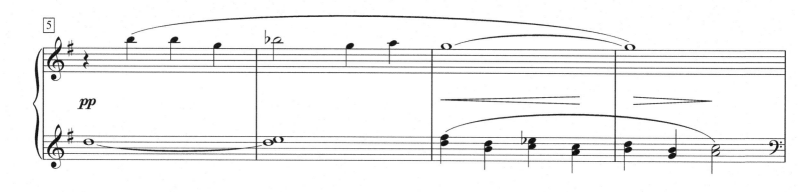

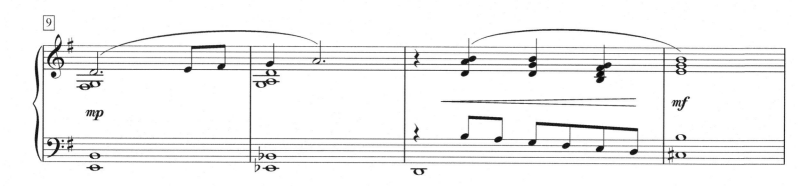

SWEET AND LOW

By JOSEPH BARNBY
Arranged by Phillip Keveren

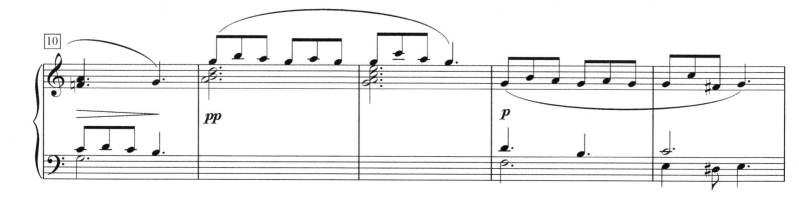

THEY DIDN'T BELIEVE ME

Words by HERBERT REYNOLDS
Music by JEROME KERN
Arranged by Phillip Keveren

Warmly, with rubato ♩= c. 96

With pedal

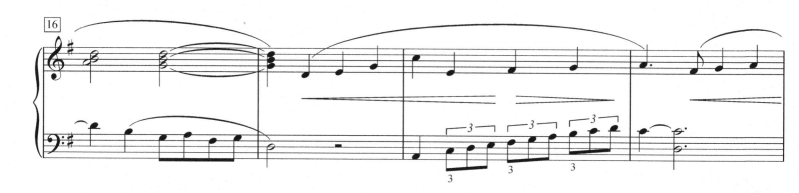

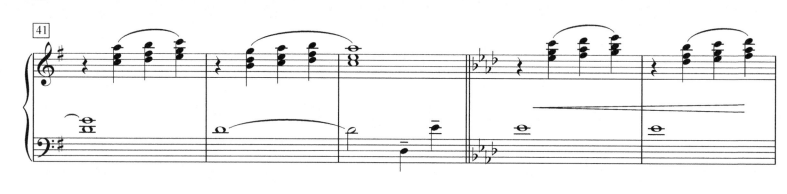

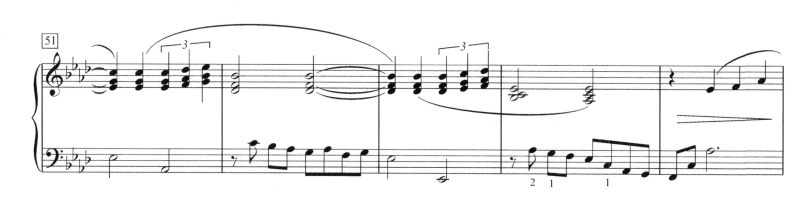

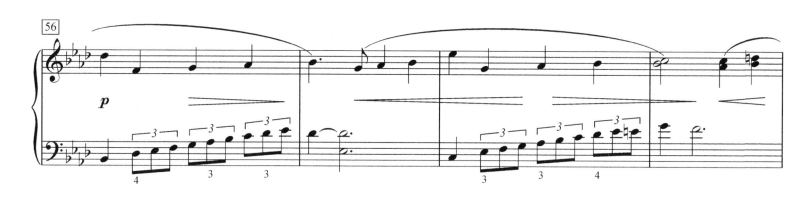

WHO'S SORRY NOW

Words by BERT KALMAR
and HARRY RUBY
Music by TED SNYDER
Arranged by Phillip Keveren

YOU MADE ME LOVE YOU
(I Didn't Want To Do It)

Words by JOE McCARTHY
Music by JAMES V. MONACO
Arranged by Phillip Keveren

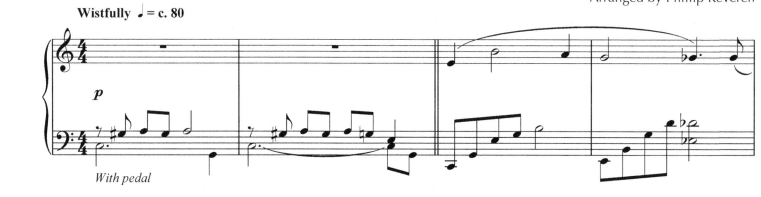

59

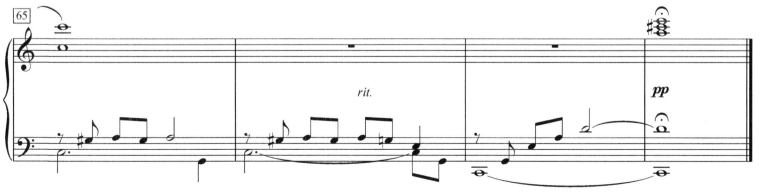

WHAT'LL I DO?

Words and Music by IRVING BERLIN
Arranged by Phillip Keveren

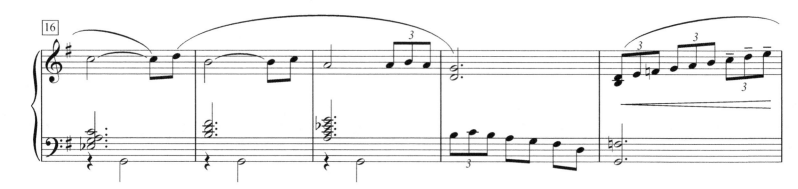